ANNIE PATCHES

My New Forever Home

ANNIE PATCHES, My New Forever Home

Story by
Marty Koblish

Photographs by Marty Koblish and
Dr. Jessica Charous, BVSc.

Copyright 2015

ISBN 13: 978-0692492055
ISBN 10: 0692492054

Published by

973-214-4246
MKA
Publishing

Books published by MKA Publishing are available for bulk purchase in the United States by corporations, institutions and other organizations. Eight inch plush "Annie calico kitties" can also be ordered to accompany any of the "Annie" books from the publisher by calling 973-214-4246.

Dedicated to Emily and Isabelle Coughlin,

ten and twelve respectively
who were the inspirations for this book
and for the book, "MAX and Annie Patches" © 2014

Profits from this book will be donated to
Neuroblastoma Research through the Jimmy Fund Walk
sponsored by the Coughlin family

My mommy lived on the streets. She had no home, no one to feed her, no one to take care of her or to love her. She was called a stray. One day she was rescued by a caring person from the animal shelter. She took my mommy to the animal hospital. A veterinarian said my mommy was going to have kittens . She found a foster family who would take care of all of us until we found our forever homes.

After I was born my mommy did not have enough milk to feed me.
My foster family fed me with a bottle until I could eat kitten kibble
by myself.

The foster family had a room that I called the play room. That is where all the foster kittens played and learned to eat by themselves.

When I was eight weeks old a wonderful family wanted to adopt me. I said goodbye to all my kitten friends and moved from New Jersey to Chatham, Massachusetts on Cape Cod.

In the beginning I lived in one room until I learned my way around. I was given lots of toys and a warm fuzzy bed. I also had lots of food and water to drink so I could grow big and strong. My food dish was bigger than I was.

I was so little and everything seemed so BIG!

I explored everything in my new room. I loved to climb up and sit in my cat tree because it made me feel taller and bigger.

My new family named me "Annie" after Little Orphan Annie and "Patches" because of my many patches of color on my fur. I Love my name "
"*Annie Patches*".

I loved to cuddle with the stuffed animals in the cradle and run through my tunnel and grab at anything that moved.

One day I jumped over the gate of my room and came down the stairs. I jumped up on a chair to look all around and hoped no one would see me.

When my family saw me, they told me that I was now ready to explore the whole house. I was so excited. There was so much to see.

I felt really cozy in the dog's food dish.

Wow, I could see myself in the bowl. It was just like a mirror.

I grew bigger everyday. My family told me I was a little cutie pie.

Peek A Boo! I see you. I had fun lying in the bowl on the dinning room table. Do you think I made a cute centerpiece?

When I was six months old I needed an operation. I came home from the veterinary hospital with a collar so I could not lick out my stitches.

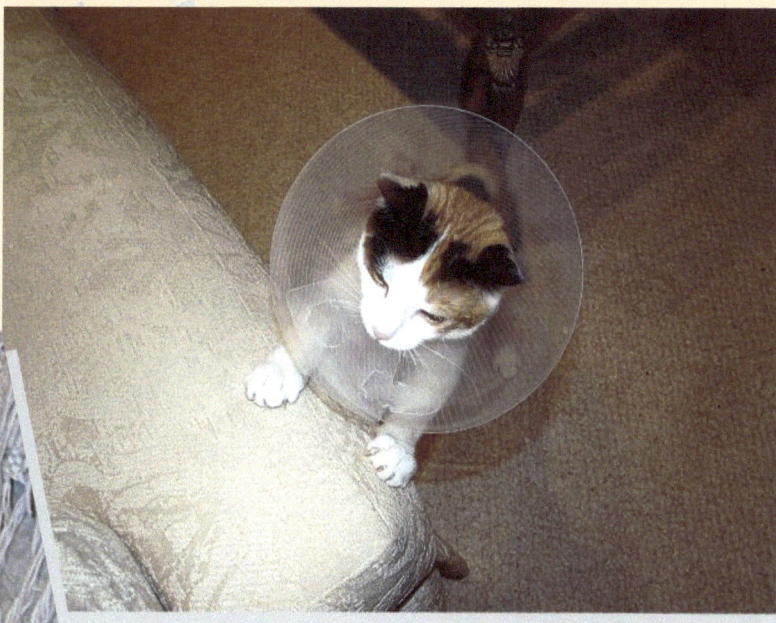

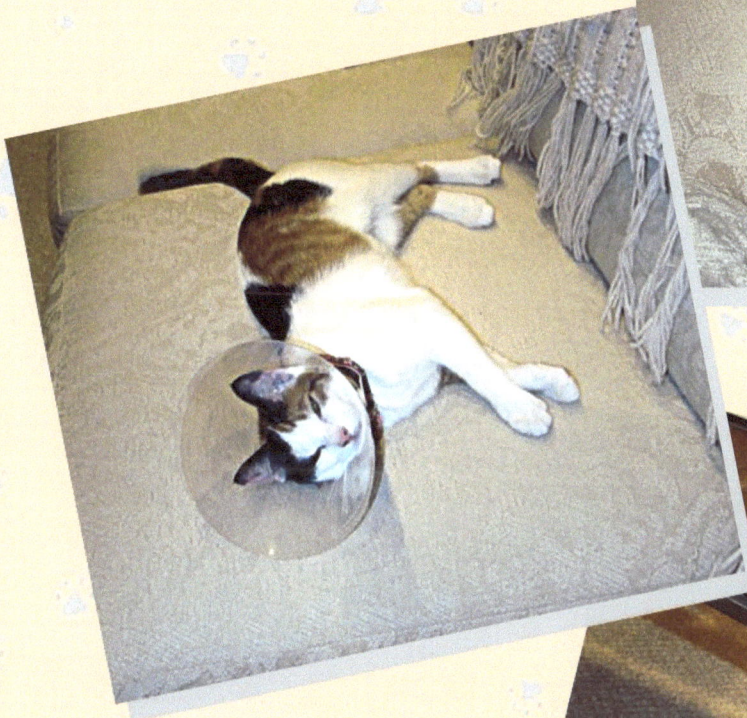

Do you think I looked cute? I loved my collar. I had fun under the coffee table pretending to be a queen.

I saw my human family wash in the sink

So I jumped in to take my bath.

When I heard my name being called, I answered right back.

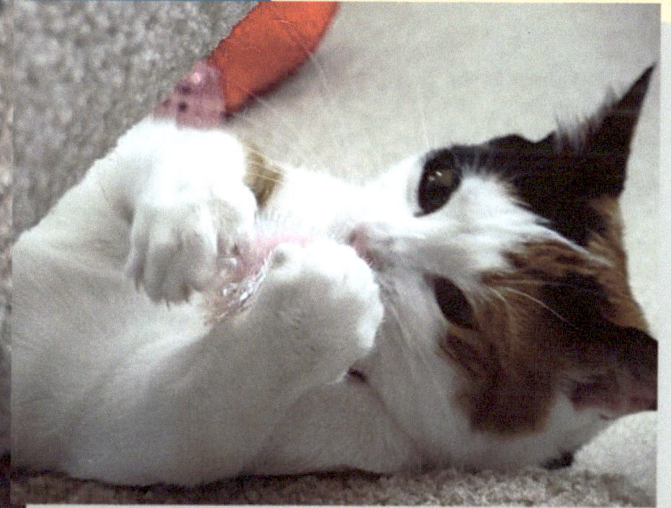

I loved to play with my catnip toys.

My First Christmas

I was given a lot of toys in my stocking.

I thought there was a mouse in there somewhere.

I could not get it out no matter how hard I tried.

I loved to lie in the sun, take naps and look out the front door.

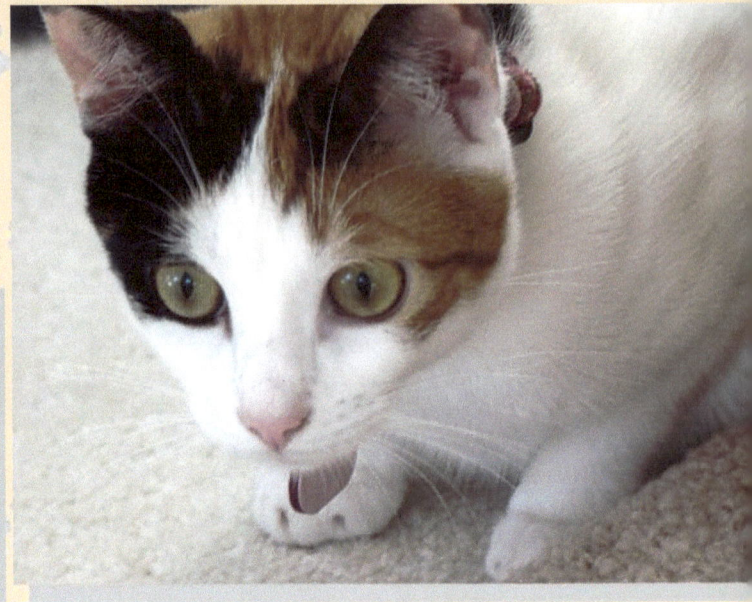

I practiced yoga and watched EVERYTHING!

One of my favorite games was to play hide and seek. Do you ever play hide and seek? On my first birthday I had fun playing hide and seek in some shopping bags.

I also liked to hide in
boxes and behind
the curtains.

In my new home I have made friends with the other pets that live there. MAX , the Betta fish and I are very different, but we find a lot of things to talk about.

When I was lonely, Bella, a Golden Retriever in my new home let me share her bed with her.

When I grew bigger, Baron, another Golden Retriever in my new home, let me play with him.

I just celebrated my seventh birthday. I was adopted by a family who loves me, brushes me, feeds me, plays with me and keeps me safe inside and healthy. My new forever home is now....my home forever!

www.ingramcontent.com/pod-product-compliance
Lightning Source LLC
Chambersburg PA
CBHW042105040426
42448CB00002B/152